DATE DUE			
MAR 19 '75 CR			
FEB 27 75 GR			

Visions of the Dusk

Fenton Johnson

Visions of the Dusk

By
Fenton Johnson

The Black Heritage Library Collection

 BOOKS FOR LIBRARIES PRESS
FREEPORT, NEW YORK
1971

First Published 1915
Reprinted 1971

Reprinted from a copy in the
Fisk University Library Negro Collection

PS 3519
.0245
V5
1971

INTERNATIONAL STANDARD BOOK NUMBER:
0-8369-8824-8

LIBRARY OF CONGRESS CATALOG CARD NUMBER:
73-161265

PRINTED IN THE UNITED STATES OF AMERICA

DEDICATION

To Dr. Albert Shaw, Jeanne Robert Foster and Josephine Turck Baker.

CONTENTS

		PAGE
1.	Prelude	1
2.	A Georgia Lullaby	2
3.	De Cabin	3
4.	The Lonely Piper	5
5.	Two Songs	6
6.	Revery	7
7.	De Ol' Home	8
8.	The Creed of the Slave	9
9.	Kin You Tell Me	10
10.	The Lost Summer	11
11.	Hymn	12
12.	The Soul of Boston	13
13.	Singing Hallelujia	14
14.	The Magic Master	15
15.	To My Father	16
16.	Howdy Do	17
17.	Lullaby	18
18.	The Soldiers of the Dusk	19
19.	Long De Cool o' Night	20
20.	The Dying Rose	21
21.	A Fragment	21
22.	De Aprul Song	22
23.	Slave Death Song	23
24.	De Call	24
25.	The Passing Indian	25
26.	Fiddlah Ike	26
27.	At the Grave of Mandy	27
28.	Jubal's Free	29

Contents

		PAGE
29.	SONG OF THE WHIRLWIND	30
30.	MY GOD IN HEAVEN SAID TO ME	31
31.	THE HYPOCRITE DEVIL	32
32.	LOVE ME	34
33.	THE PRODIGAL SONG	35
34.	THE SONG OF BEULAHLAND	37
35.	DE BAN'	37
36.	PLANTATION SERMON	38
37.	THE PHANTOM RABBIT	39
38.	TO JEANNE ROBERT FOSTER	40
39.	S. COLERIDGE TAYLOR	40
40.	ETHIOPIA	42
41.	DE CHU'CH	48
42.	DE MULE	50
43.	QUESTIONS	51
44.	LYRICS OF LOVE	51
45.	WHEN APRIL COMES	54
46.	THE CLINGING KISS	55
47.	EULOGY ON THE FAIRIES	56
48.	MEMORIES	58
49.	WHEN MY BONNIE DANCES	58
50.	MARY ON AUGUST THE FIRST	60
51.	DOUGLAS	60
52.	OL' AGE	62
53.	THE WRAITHIES' MESSAGE	63
54.	WASHIN' DAY	64
55.	AT THE SHRINE OF MARY	65
56.	A PILGRIM OF THE DUSK	67
57.	DEATH	67
58.	WARNING	68
59.	DECLARATION	68
60.	TURN DOWN THE LAMP	69
61.	COMIN' HOME	70
62.	L'ENVOI	71

FOREWORD.

Mr. Johnson is a young colored poet of America; some of his verse is in formal cultivated English, some in the corrupted language of the American negro. The latter rings true; it expresses with singular intensity the joys an sorrows of a subject race.—
Literary World (London) April 2, 1914.

A slender book of verse, "A Little Dreaming" is the work of Mr. Fenton Johnson, a young Negro poet, born in Chicago in 1888 and educated at the University of Chicago and the Northwestern University. He has written short stories and dramas of Negro life and considerable lyric verse. "A Little Dreaming" gives promise of a true poetic gift, a natural, spontaneous lyricism with the same distinguishing racial qualities that characterise the work of Paul Lawrence Dunbar. Many of the lines are melodious with the primitive, plaintive reediness of the Negro "Spirituals" of slave days. The chant-like form is effectively used, as in his lament for Dunbar.

American Review of Reviews, January 1914.

Visions of the Dusk.

PRELUDE.

'Tis twilight dim; the musing dreamer sits
Before his hearth, the sunset on his brow,
And thus he ponders ere the birth of dusk.

Some love the land where grew the laurel tree,
The home of Gods and stern faced warriors,
The altar Nature built and Art preserves;
And long to hear heroic note from Pan.
Such deem their love the freeborn English note,
And others love the freeborn English note,
The music of the songs the lusty sang
In Mermaid Tavern and the Old Boar's Head,
The gift of Shakespeare and the heritage
Of Tennyson, the child romance hath nursed.

And yet some say to me, "O Man of Dusk,
Give us thy songs in broken Afric tongue,—
The music o fthe peasant in the South—
The native strain alone is poetry.
Be thou as Burns or Dunbar was,
Be thou as Lowell in his adobe home;
The humble peasant is the truest bard."

'Tis not in classic mould or English flame,
Or lilting song from crudest peasant tongue
The soul that seeks the beauty of a truth

VISIONS OF THE DUSK.

Can gaze upon the ever gleaming light
That flickers on the summit Poesy.
But 'tis in living and the wonder Life
We find the soul of Beauty is a God;
The vision is the thing, and not the word.
Then come with me where Life and Soul hath met;
And hear the mother-croon of far-away,
The dying note of Georgia lullaby.

VISIONS OF THE DUSK.

A GEORGIA LULLABY.

1.

Sleep, my honey, dreaming time is here,
Fancy in her barge is drifting near,
In the slumb'ring pine the birdie sings
To the weary charge beneath her wings.
Sleep, my honey, sleep to-night, to-night.

2.

Lay your head upon my heaving breast;
From my soul I grant you peace and rest;
Never sandman come to wake my child
With a melody so strangely wild.
Sleep, my honey, sleep to-night, to-night.

Visions of the Dusk.

DE CABIN.

1.

Now have you nevah seed jes' whar we stayed
W'en we war jes' erbout so very high?
'Twas whar bluegrass am growin' 'side de do'
An' rabbits go a-la'kin' o' de hill,
'Twas in de cabin whar mah Mammy lived
An' Daddy, too,—de blessed man ob Gawd—
Jes' on de othah side de Cunnel's house
An' bac' de fiel' whar growed de cotton flowah.
Go talk erbout yo' mansions made o' brick,
Go holler 'bout yo' lawn dat's green an' wide,
You kain't mak' me fu'git mah ol', ol' home,
Whar Mammy wu'ked an' Mammy lived an' died.
'Twas jes' some bo'ds an' plastah, too,
All put tegethah in a so't o' way
Dat mak' you know d'aint no othah house
Jes' lak de cabin dat ol' Daddy built.
But sweat an' sass an' hungah was de price
We paid tuh git dat sheltuh on its feet.
Mah Daddy built it by de bright moonlight
W'en all his wu'k wid-in de fiel' was done,
An' weddah goblins he'ped him Ah kain't say,
But nevah had a da'ky such a home.
Erroun' de stoop mah Mammy trained huh vines,
An' in de ya'd dey growed de violet,

VISIONS OF THE DUSK.

De honeysuckle an' de roses, too,
An' o' them towahed sweet magnolia tree.
De lily ob de valley lingahed neah,
An' nigh dem all pealed fo'th de mockin' bu'd.
(Go 'way! Ah wish mah soul dat Ah was daih.)
W'en ebenin' come, an' all de wu'k was done,
Mah Daddy stacked his hoe, an' et his meal
Wid me an' Sukey, Sam an' Viney, too,
An' Mammy puttin' fo'th huh cookin' good—
De sweetin' 'taters brown ez Dinah's cheeks,
De 'possum grinnin' in his gravy thick,
An' hoecake, hot an' sweet an' greasy, too,
An' Daddy say his blessin', "O, good Lawd,
Gib all de worl' jes' what You gib to us"
An' Mammy add, "A-men!" f'un out huh hea't.
An' w'en ouah stomachs bulged jes' lak de pigs
We sat o' played upon de cabin stoop;
Ol' Daddy picked his banjo: "Hum!—Ti!—Tum!"
An' sing, "Mah Susy, Susy, Susy Gal,
You's sweetuh dan de honey on de vine".
An' Mammy say, "You sho's a funny man,
Go 'long! You ain't a-talkin' 'bout dis chile".
An' fo' we laid upon ouah baids o' straw
Ol' Daddy'd git upon his knees an' pray,
"Good Lawd, keep all mah folks f'um ha'm an' hu't;
Mah wife, mah chillun, an' mah Mestah, too."
Mah Daddy nevah read no book but one,
Mah Mammy nevah knowed no book but one,
An' dat was allus on de cabin she'f.

Visions of the Dusk.

De book dat Jesus wrote—de Book o' Books.
Mah Daddy sleeps beside de cabin do',
Mah Mammy lies beneaf de violets,
Po' Sukey, Sam an' Viney's gone away,
De banjo's crumblin' quick to ash an' dust,
An Ah is lonely, lonely in de worl'.
O folks dat see me sottin' on de stone,
Please drop me coin an' let me gwi' away
To whar my cabin gleams beneaf de sun.

THE LONELY PIPER.

1.
Tell me, lonely piper by the stream,
With your pipe of wond'rous melody,
Why alone sit you and pipe all day
When the gold lies near, and gold is fame?

2.
I am piping for the love of song,
For the sunset and the rise of moon;
I am piping for the summer wind
That hath come afar to hear my strain.

3.
I am piping for a little child,
Sleeping on a couch beneath the earth.
Oh, I hope some day he hears my song,
And comes leaping forth to greet the dawn.

Visions of the Dusk.

TWO SONGS.
I.

THE SONG OF THE PASSING.

1.
I am weary of this loving and this grieving,
Lay me down beneath the bending willows,
Strew upon me petals of the bleeding roses,
   O my mourners.

2.
I am weary of this loving and this sighing,
Bring me sweet Aljulia ere I meet the boatman
By the shining waters of the mystic river,
   O my mourners.

3.
Let me hear the breezes singing low of Heaven,
Let me feel the cool of earth upon my body,
Let me hear the laughter of the little children,
   O my mourners.

II.

I am the dusk,
The dreamborn soul
   Of yesterday;
I am the hope
Of true Love's birth,—
   The Man in Chains.

Visions of the Dusk.

2.

I am the star
Whose light descends
    Beneath the sea;
I am the rose
Whose perfume lives
    Beyond the years.

3.

I am thy rod,
I am thy staff,
    O brothers pale;
For thee I live,
For thee I die,
    O brothers mine.

REVERY.

1.

I was the starlight,
I was the moonlight,
I was the sunset,
Before the dawning
    Of my life;
I was the river
Forever winding
To purple dreaming,
I was the glowing
Of youthful Springtime,

VISIONS OF THE DUSK.

I was the singing
Of golden songbirds,—
  I was love.

2.

I was the sunlight,
I was the twilight,
I was the humming
Of winged creatures
  Ere my birth;
I was the blushing
Of lily maiden,
I was the vision
Of youthful striving,
I was the summer,
I was the autumn,
I was the All-time—
  I was love.

DE OL' HOME.

1.

Ah's longin' fu' de ol' home far away,
Whar Mammy lies beside de glidin' crick;
Ah's longin' fu' de lan' o' summer day,
Whar lillies ob-de valley's mighty thick;
Ah's longin' fu' tuh feel de bayou bref
Sof'ly blowin' on dis cheek o' mine;
Ah's longin' fu' de honey dat ah lef',
Awaitin' me whar grows de ol' giant pine.

VISIONS OF THE DUSK.

2.

De earf am weary, an' Ah's sick at hea't,
Ah wish dat ah could be away down home;
Ah's played up hyeah a rovin', lovin' paht,
Been eb'rywhere de face ob man is known,
But only whar in pickanniny day
Ah romped an' to' an' ate de sugahcane
Can Ah be happy all de res' de day—
Down at mah ol', ol' home in Mandy Lane!

THE CREED OF THE SLAVE.

1.

Ah lubs de worl'.—Kain't he'p it, dat's mah way.
Futh'mo' Ah lubs de night, Ah lubs de day,
Ah lubs de suff'rin' crittuhs dat Gawd made,
De li'l 'uns playin' 'neaf de locus' shade,
Ah lubs de shadduhs by de gret big road,
Ah lubs to tote wid me de hebby load
Thoo'all de live long night an' thoo' de day.
Ah lubs de worl'.—Kain't he'p it, dat's mah way.

2.

Go crack yo' whups, an' break dis flesh o' mine,
Ah ain't a-gwine tuh, leave dis love behin';
Ah wu'k an' bleed fu' dose dat hu't me mos',
But in de mawnin' w'en Ah am a ghos'
Ah pray de Lawd dat you kin come up daih

Visions of the Dusk.

An' play wid me erpon de golden staih.
Ah lubs you all, po' suff'rin' clay;—
Ah lubs de worl'.—Kain't he'p it, dat's mah way.

KIN YOU TELL ME?

1.

Sukey Jane, you sho' is gittin' wise,
Gwine tuh school, an' usin' bofe yo' eyes,
You know mo' dan Brudder Gabrul knows,
You kin tell de whyness ob de rose,
You kin figger out de gleamin' stahs,
An' go talkin' 'bout yo' flamin' Mahs.
But, mah honey, listen!—listen close!
Kin you tell me whaih de ol' moon goes
W'en de daytahm thoo' de valley glows?

2.

Sukey Jane, you knows mos' evahthing,
Jes' why robin sings his bes' in Spring,
You kin tell de why ob day an' night,
An' jes' why de bu'ds dey mak' daih flight,
You kin read de books ob long ago,
But, mah honey, listen!—listen close!
Kin you tell me whaih dey keeps de rose
W'en de wintuh thoo' de valley blows?

Visions of the Dusk.

THE LOST SUMMER.

(SONG)

1.

Where is summer, now the rose is dead?
Where is summer, now the birds have fled?
I have wandered at the dusk of day,
But have never found the flowers of May.

2.

Where is summer, now that I am old?
Where is summer, now my love is cold?
Years have dropt their frost upon my brow,
And the warmth of youth is fleeing now.

Dearest, you were summertime to me,
Youth and beauty 'neath a maple tree,
I have mourned for you when Night was young,
I have sighed for you where stars are hung,
But you left my heart in days gone by
But you let my hope of true love die.
Lovely hour of bloom, I long for thee!
Dear, lost summertime, return to me!

Visions of the Dusk.

HYMN.

1.

Great God of a million years,
Bulwark of our ancient fears,
    Lead us on;
Sorrows come and sorrows go,
But Thy comfort nations know;
Princes, lords, and captains fall,
But the lowly hear thy call;
    Lead us on.

2.

'Cross the tide the storms may blow,
Fires of evil brightly glow,
    Lead us on;
When around us thrives the night
Burn anew, O Starry Light,
Let the moaning sea-winds die
Ere the angel Love pass by;
    Lead us on.

3.

Nations marching to the Cross,
On their hearts the Sign emboss,
    Lead us on;
By Thy hand the fallen rise
To the glory of the skies ,

Visions of the Dusk.

By Thy hand a thousand years
Thou shalt dry our earthly tears;
Lead us on.

THE SOUL OF BOSTON.

My cobblestones are red with England's blood,
My parks are monuments of other days,
My battle cry the cry that right is might,
Humanity my God and mother love.
I blush when Justice cowers i nthe dust,
When once again we lead to Calvary
The Nazarene enwrapt in scarlet cloak.
I am the sister of the man oppressed,
The sword that flashed at primal Eden's gate,
"No man may enter save the pure in heart".
I sit at Plato's feet, and glean the gold
That drifts from such a rich eternal mind;
Good England's culture is my fading past,
Columbia the glory of my dreams.
O sisters mine, go sound your drums of gold,
Go build your monuments to Greed and Pelf,
For I would rather cherish martyrs' blood
Than all the wealth enshrined in Amsterdam,
And I would rather boast the motherhood
Of Attucks and of Shaw than rule the world.
O God of Winthrop, here I spread Thy couch,
For I have kept Thy faith despite the age.

VISIONS OF THE DUSK.

SINGING HALLELUJIA.

(A Negro Spiritual)

1.

I went down to Jordan,
    Singing, "Hallelujia!",
I went down to Jordan
    In the nighttime;
God of mine above me,
God of mine beneath me,
And the white robed angels
    Singing, "Hallelujia!"

2.

I looked up to Heaven,
    Singing, "Hallelujia",
I looked up to Heaven
    In the nighttime;
God poured down His mercy,
Christ poured down His loving,
And the choir of angels
    Sang me, "Hallelujia!"

3.

Threescore stood in Heaven,
    Singing, "Hallelujia",
Threescore stood in Heaven
    In the nighttime;

Visions of the Dusk.

David with his captains,
Jesus with His fishers,
And the white robed angels
    Singing, "Hallelujia!"
4.
Take me swift to Heaven,
    Singing, "Hallelujia!"
Take me swift to Heaven
    In the nighttime;
Seat me 'mid the lillies,
Crown me with the roses,
And let whiterobed angels
    Sing me, "Hallelujia."

THE MAGIC MASTER.

I am the Magic Master,
The mighty twilight weaver;
Before my tent the vision
In youthful splendour dances,
From mountains tinged with jasper
Bring I the sunlight glowing,
From forest tinged with dusk light
Bring I the moonlight lantern.
My magic is my dreaming,
My dreaming is my loving;
I know the warm Sahara,
I know the cool Alaska,

Visions of the Dusk.

I know the rose hued peri
Before my couch in Heaven;
I climb the golden stairways
Within my ears the singing
Of angels crowned with haloes,
Before my eyes the laurel
Ye give the wizard dying.
At Camelot with Merlin,
With Israfel in Heaven,
Among the dusky minstrels
In fields of waving cotton
Learned I the gift of magic;
And now that day is dying
I watch my star descending
Into the deathless river,
For now I know that magic
Will live beyond the starlight.

TO MY FATHER.

1.

Good Father o' the Dusk, my love for thee
Is boundless as the soul's eternal sea;
Thou wrought for me when I was weak and young,
And guarded me from life's tempestuous wrong.

2.

Thou art the lamp that safely pilots me
Beyond the crags and shoals of life's rough sea;

VISIONS OF THE DUSK.

I cannot falter when thou bidst me go
Where moonlit waters to the ocean flow.

3.

Let others boast of gold and mansions grand,
No father lives throughout this Western land
So good, so true, so brave of heart as thee,
My mariner across the starlit sea.

HOWDY DO.

1.

Oh, de runnin' crick he say to me,
    "Howdy do' mah honey, howdy do;
An' de bu'ds dey sing f'um top de tree,
    "Howdy do, mah honey, howdy do."
Oh, de cunnin' rabbit grin an' say,
    "Howdy do, mah honey, howdy do,"
But de' possum hidin' 'fraid to say,
    "Howdy do, mah honey, howdy do.'

2.

Oh, Miss Sally say to me las' night.
    "Howdy do, mah honey, howdy do,"
An, Ah say to huh, mah eyes so bright,
    "Howdy do, mah honey, howdy do."
Oh, de win's a croonin' thoo de trees,
    "Howdy do, mah honey, howdy do,"
An' f'um hives de buzzin' ob de bees,
    "Howdy do, mah honey, howdy do."

VISIONS OF THE DUSK.

3.

Oh, de owl's a hootin' all night long
    "Howdy do, mah honey, howdy do,"
An' de mockin' bu'd he sings de song
    "Howdy do, mah honey, howdy do."
F'um behin' de clouds de moon she say,
    "Howdy do, mah honey, howdy do,"
An' de Night she whispuh to de Day,
    "Howdy do, mah honey, howdy do."

LULLABY.

1.

Bye lo, mah li'l lam',
In de locus' swingin';
Bye lo, mah li'l lam',
Mammy by you singin',
Shadders am a-creepin',
F'um de clouds a-peepin',
Wants tuh see li'l lady,
Wants tuh see brown baby
    In de locus' tree.

2.

Bye lo, mah li'l lam',
Cool o' night's a-comin';
Bye lo, mah li'l lam',
Katy-did's a-hummin';
All de worl' am sleepin',

Visions of the Dusk.

    Gawd yo' soul am keepin',
    Angels o'er you beamin',
    Bringing you sweet dreamin',
      In de locus' tree.

THE SOLDIERS OF THE DUSK.
I.
Black men holding up the earth,
Atlas burdened they descend
Deep into the vale of Hell;
And with valor long defend
Fairer brothers from the wounds
That the dogs of war inflict,
And with patriotic souls
Die in Europe's last conflict.

II.
Paris shall not fall so long
As there breathes a man of dusk,
London shall be saved an age
By the fighters of the dusk;
Zulu, robbed of land and home,
For the robber bares his heart,
Kaffir, giving Europe gems,
Europe pierces with a dart.

III.
They are pagan, men of blood,
They have not a golden rule,
Cannibals and fetish men
With their laws intensely cruel;

VISIONS OF THE DUSK.

But the God of Calvary
Will in years unborn be just
To the men who died for men,
Victims of the war god's lust.

'LONG DE COOL O' NIGHT.

1.

'Long de cool o' night w'en day am daid,
An' de wu'k am done, mah pipe Ah smokes
On de cabin stoop wid Mandy nigh,
Laffin' fit tuh kill at all mah jokes;
Pickanninies tumblin' in de san',
Kickin' up daih heels wid ka'less joy,
Totin' back tuh me de happy days
W'en lak dem Ah was a ba'hfoot boy.

2.

Let de 'skeeters hum 'way an' de owl
Go a-tootin' in de gread, big tree;
Let de moon go dippin' in de sky,
Whituh dan de spray f'um out de sea;
Ah is gwine tuh sit upon de stoop
Wid mah Mandy in de bright moonlight
Holdin' han's an' co'tin' huh ag'in,
Kase its lovin' tahm an' cool o' night.

VISIONS OF THE DUSK.

THE DYING ROSE.

1.

The rose lay dying in the summer heat
And longed to save her life so fair and brief.
A dryad, bathing in the noonday sun,
Spied her and dropped a tear to show her grief.
The panting bloom drank deep the sweetening drop—
And lived an hour to deck a singer's wreath.

A FRAGMENT.

1.

One sunset when the skies were deepest red,
As if they blushed for all the human sins,
I saw her gather daffodils, and sighed,
For she was sweeter far than those poor flowers
And all the flowers that grace this universe,
And in my dream I saw a crown descend
From out the firmament and drop to earth.
It fell beside a brook whose gleaming drops
Shone like the diamonds in the sable night,
And I, the humblest in the realm of men,
Stooped low and placed it on her bonny head.

Visions of the Dusk.

DE APRUL SONG.

1.

Lets go out a la'kin', jes' to-day,
Livin's tiahsome, 'doubt dey let you play;
Fishin's good, an' plenty bait's erroun',
Now dat springtime's sproutin' f'om de groun';
Possum want a bullet in his hide,
Rabbit say he wish you'd pierce his side;
Dis am jus' de time fu' man to shu'k,
W'en de Aprul sunshine spiles yo' wuk.

2.

Sweet magnoly bloomin' on de trees,
Apple blossom thick wid honey bees,
Lillies ob de valley noddin' way
Whisp'rin', "Dis am sho' a lubby day!"
Crissy green a sproutin' by de do',
Lilacs eb'rywhaih am' boun' to grow;
Dis am jes' de time fu' man to shu'k
W'en de Aprul goodness spiles yo' wu'k.

3.

Mockin' bu'd a-singin' on de hill,
Sunshine drappin' down into de rill,
Cotton sprout a peepin' f'om de earf,
Raccoons runnin' 'roun' chuck full o' mirf,

VISIONS OF THE DUSK.

Co'npone cookin' on de cabin harf,
Pickanninnes playin' on de wharf;
Dis am jes' de time fu' man to shu'k
W'en de Aprul gladness spiles yo' wu'k.

SLAVE DEATH SONG.

1.

Oh, my chariot is swinging,
    Jesus, bring it near,
Soft I hear the harp a-ringing,
    Jesus, bring it near,
All my troubles are a-dying,
Low within the grave a-lying,
Angels o'er my bones a-bending,
Peace and rest to me descending;
    Jesus, bring it near,

2.

Throne of God is shining brightly,
    Jesus, bring it near,
Angels stepping round it sprightly,
    Jesus, take me home.
Curved coach with jasper cover
Swinging for the dusky lover;
White robed choir is sweetly singing,
Glory music earthward bringing,
    Jesus, take me home.

Visions of the Dusk.

3.

Scythe of Heaven gently reaping,
    Jesus, bring it near,
Love eternal o'er me creeping,
    Jesus, bring it near;
  Day within the West is dying,
O'er me summer breeze is sighing,
    To my mother's breast returning,
    For me long she has been yearning;
    Jesus, take me home.

DE CALL.

1.

Ah's moughty lonely 'thout you' honey chile,
Be'n down to Bubbly's Crick, an' mo'ned awhile,
Walked thoo de fiel' ob co'n, an' drapped a teah;
An' tol' de jaybu'ds dat Ah wished you heah;
De rabbit run no mo', but look fo' you,
De owl he cry all night, "Tu-whoo! Tu-whoo!
Come bac', come bac', we wants you honey chile!"

2.

De bu'ds dey chu'p no mo' daih songs ob cheah,
Dey seem tuh say dey wish dat you whar neah,
De chillun hang hang daih haids, an' wonduh why
No mo' you pass de ol' plantation by,
De banjo's silent now, de fiddle still,

Visions of the Dusk.

No mo' de dawgs go huntin' o' de hill:
Come bac', come bac', we wants you honey chile!

3.

All night mah pillo's wet wid teahs Ah drap,
Yo' cu'ly lock Ah fondle in mah lap,
Ah's longin' moughty ha'd fu' days gone by
W'en mammy seed de lovelight in yo' eye;
De day it seem jes' lak a sack ob co'n,
De night's de lonlies' since Ah was bo'n;
Come bac', come bac', we wants you honey chile!

THE PASSING INDIAN.

1.

By the shore of lonely Long Ago,
By the waters of Forgetfulness,
Wrapped in woven blanket stained with blood
Stand I gazing at the dying tribes;
In my hand the ancient tomahawk,
In my eye a fire that never dies,
But soars high to Gitchie Manitou
As the eagle flies at eventide.
O thou race of squaws, be kind to me;
Let me smoke with thee the calumet,
Let me hunt the bison and the deer,
Let me breathe the air of libery
In the land the white man's blossom choked,
Ere the purple sunset calls me home.

Visions of the Dusk.

2.

I am dying as the wounded deer,
I who once was master of these shores;
Might and brawn I held my majesty,
Infinite I deemed this strength of mine,
Morning star and sunset glow my God;
Passion ruled within this breast of mine,
And before me swept my better self.
Listen, O thou mighty race of squaws,
Ere the purple sunset calls me home;
Thou may pass away as I have passed—
Gitchie Manitou alone is Chief,
Sachem of the mighty Winds is He,
And He lives till dry the stream of Time.
Be not vain, but hear His gentle voice,
O my worthy brothers pale of face,
Ere the purple sunset calls thee home.

FIDDLAH IKE.

1.

Oh' Fiddlah Ike's a-playin' to de moon
Erbout his wife dat died away las' June.
He play de saddes' tune in all de worl'
"Oh, whaih's mah honey? Whaih's mah Pearl?"
An' down his cheek he drap a shiny teah,
Fu' Liza was his honey an' his deah.

Visions of the Dusk.

2.

De hull plantation gathuh roun' his do',
An' w'en he play daih haids go drappin' low,
De houn' dawg quit his howlin' all de night,
De lonely moon put on huh brightes' light,
Fu' all de worl' would lak to heah de chune
Dat Fiddlah Ike's been playin' thoo de June.

3.

Ol' Marstuh's stop his drinkin' spahklin' wine
An' come a-pushin' bac' good Mammy's vine,
"Its Fiddlah Ike!" he says, "Go play yo' bes',
Yo' Lizas up above in Glohry's dress,
She's lookin' down, and heahs yo' fiddle song,
A sobbin' way thoo out de ebenin' long."

4.

Dey say de angels come thoo sorrer's gate,
Dat music's sweetes' when you's lost yo' mate,
Dey say de golden th'one was nevah won
By livin' all de time beneaf de sun;
An' dat's de reason Ike kin move de worl'
A playin', "Whaih's mah honey? Whaih's mah Pearl?"

AT THE GRAVE OF MANDY.

1.

Mandy's sleepin' wid de angels now—
Mandy dat was sweetes' ob dem all—
An' we laid huh side de hic'ry tree

Visions of the Dusk.

'Till de day she heah huh Mastah's call:
Ah kin feel huh ahms erroun' mah nec',
Ah kin feel de puffume ob huh bref;
An' de teahs go tumblin' down mah cheeks,
Kase de folkses call huh sleepin' def.

2.

Did you evah see mah Mandy, chile?
Lawd! but she was diffunt f'um de res',
Eyes dat's blackuh dan de blackes' night,
Teef dat's whituh dan a chicken's bres';
You should felt dose han's, wahm an' sof',
You should tas'e dem lips dat tas'e lak mo',
Den you'd know fu' sho' de reason why
Ah am allus lingerin' by huh do'.

3.

Buhds may sing daih songs, an' sing 'em well,
Brook go laffin' lak ol' sorrer's daid,
Rabbit grin, an' possum hol' his sides,
An' de owl go shake his wise ol' haid;
But daih's nuffin' will be chee'ful now,
All de earf am but a lonely lan',
While mah Mandy's in de Beulahlan'
Singin' 'Glory' wid de angel ban'.

NEGRO SPIRITUALS.

(These songs we offer, not as genuine Negro spirituals, but as imitations. We attempt to preserve the

VISIONS OF THE DUSK.

rhythm and the spirit of the slaves, and to give a literary form and interpretation to their poetic endeavour. Here and there we have caught a phrase the unlettered minstrels used; here and there we have borrowed of that exquisite Oriental imagery the Africans brought with them.

JUBAL'S FREE.

1.

Sound the trumpet, honey,
    Jubal's free,
Sound the ram horn, honey,
    Jubal's free;
Devil goes a-quaking,
Mighty Hell is shaking,
All the stars are tumbling,
Heaven's thunder rumbling,
    Jubal's free.

2.

Dance the Gospel, honey,
    Jubal's free,
Set your feet a-swinging
    Jubal's free;
Night has changed to morning,
In her breast the warning
Of the God of sorrow,
"They must go to-morrow",
    Jubal's free.

Visions of the Dusk.

3.

Ring the church bells, honey,
    Jubal's free;
Set the chimes a-pealing,
    Jubal's free;
God above is shouting,
Devil goes a-pouting,
Earth and sky is meeting,
Freedom is their greeting,
    Jubal's free.

4.

Shake the hand, my brother.
    Jubal's free,
Sing your loudest, brother,
    Jubal's free;
Toss your head to Heaven,
Living's like the leaven,
Earth is rich with sunlight,
Night is rich with moonlight,
    Jubal's free.

SONG OF THE WHIRLWIND.

1.

Oh, my God is in the whirlwind,
    I am walking in the valley;
Lift me up, O Shining Father,
To the glory of the heavens,
I have seen a thousand troubles

Visions of the Dusk.

On the journey men call living,
I have drunk a thousand goblets
From misfortune's bitter winepress,
But to Thee I cling forever,
God of Jacob, God of Rachel.

2.

Oh, my soul is in the whirlwind,
    I am dying in the valley,
Oh, my soul is in the whirlwind
And my bones are in the valley;
At her spinning wheel is Mary
Spinning raiment of the lillies,
On her knees is Martha honey
Shining bright the golden pavement,
All the ninety nine is waiting
For my coming, for my coming.

MY GOD IN HEAVEN SAID TO ME.

1.

My God in Heaven said to me,
"Your mansion's ready in the sky,
Come home, my weary wanderer,
And eat with Me the bread of life,
For I have slain the fatted calf,
For I have filled the honey bowl
And thou shalt always dwell with me.
Come home, my weary wanderer,"
My God in Heaven said to me.

Visions of the Dusk.

2.

And now I board the Gospel train,
For I am going home to-night
To meet my God on Jordan's coast.
My burdens to the wind I toss,
To-morrow freedom shall be mine;—
A golden crown with burning stars,
And harp of David in my hand
That I may chant the Gospel tunes.

3.

On God's plantation I shall dwell,
The overseer of happiness,
And dance with Israel the dance
Of holiness and righteousness,
A thousand years with God to dwell
Is like a holiday below;
And Oh, my heart was glad to hear
My God in Heaven say to me,
"Your mansion's ready in the sky."

THE HYPOCRITE DEVIL.

1.

The Devil is a mighty hypocrite,
He steals away your heart, he steals your soul,
He rides you straight to Hell with honey words,
Oh, yes! That Devil's mighty hypocrite.

Visions of the Dusk.

2.
Last night he said to me, "My daughter, dance!
Go shuffle on the old barn floor your feet,
Nobody looking but the moon and stars.
Go shuffle on the old barn floor your feet."

3.
I looked me straight to East and straight to West,
And from my trunk I took my yellow dress,
That I might dance once more the sinner's dance
Before my bones grew old and cold and stiff.

4.
But ere I reached the barnyard gate I saw
My God of Jacob shining in the sky
"Go back, my daughter, to your pots and pans!
Dance not the sinner's dance lest ye should die."

5.
He dipped my soul in water pure with love,
And led me homeward by the magic star,
"Beware!" He said. "The Devil's conjure man;
A mighty conjure man and hypocrite."

6.
O children o fthe King, give heed to me
Go not with Beezlebub and all his ways,
Stay home and work your patch before you die,
The Devil's hypocrite and conjure man.

Visions of the Dusk.

LOVE ME.

1.

Love me, love me evermore,
    Oh, my honey! Oh, my honey!
Love me till the Judgment Day,
    Oh, my honey! Oh, my honey!
When the angel sounds the call
Hold my hand and hold it long
I will guide thee o'er the tide
To the Throne of God Himself,
    Oh, my honey! Oh, my honey!

2.

Love me, love me evermore,
    Oh, my honey! Oh, my honey!
Love me through the ages long,
    Oh, my honey! Oh, my honey!
Kiss my brow when life is cold
And a-down the stream I float,
Lift me from the ways of earth
To the warmth of God Himself,
    Oh, my honey! Oh, my honey!

3.

Love me, love me evermore,
    Oh, my honey! Oh, my honey!
Love me till the stream runs dry,
    Oh, my honey! Oh, my hone!

VISIONS OF THE DUSK.

Thrice a thousand times to die
Would be like a day with God
If that dying would bring thee
To my heart a single hour,
    Oh, my honey! Oh, my honey!

THE PRODIGAL SON.

1.

Snow is on the earth,
Sunshine in the heaven,
Snow is on the earth
And my soul a-stumbling,
Night is calling soft,
"Bring me home the weary",
God commands the host,
"Kill the fatted heifer,
    For my son is coming home."

2.

Peter holds the key,
David's voice is golden,
Simeon is praying;
In my chariot
I am drawing nigher
To the Mercy Seat
Of the shining Father
In the Land of Golden Hours.

Visions of the Dusk.

3.

Rachel cooks the Lamb,
Mary weaves me raiment,
Moses writes my name,
Joshua is shouting,
All the host rejoice
For my late returning;
Jesus takes my hand,
Calling me his brother
From the Land of Golden pain.

4.

Dark my home on earth,
Bright the Glory cabin,
Dark my home on earth,
Bright the streets of Heaven,
Never whip nor lash,
Never bread and water,
Parted on the cruel block
Waits the sainted mother
For the coming of her son.

5.

Speed thy lissome oar,
Oh, my valiant boatman,
Speed o'er Jordan's stream,
To the Land of Shining Glory.

VISIONS OF THE DUSK.

THE SONG OF BEULAHLAND.

1.

Oh, I know a river where your troubles flow,
    Down by Beulahland;
There the children of the King shall meet their Lord,
    Down by Beulahland;
Oh, I know the weapon that those children wield,
'Tis the Cross of Jesus pierced on Calvary,
And my weary soul is clinging to the beams
    Down by Beulahland.

2.

Let me not go there by fiddle tune or harp,
    Down by Beulahland,
Play no banjo on my journey to the King,
    Down by Beulahland,
Let me fight my battles in the way I choose
I alone must win the crown of Righteousness,
Let me be a soldier with my armor on,
    Down by Beulahland.

DE BAN'.

Don't you heah de ban', Miss Mandy Lee?
Don't you see de leadah wave to me?
How dose da'kies ma'ch if to wo',
Fo'teen strong, all bright wid music's glow;

VISIONS OF THE DUSK.

Daih is Eph un Jackson, drummah boy,
Wid dose sticks he's beatin' scrumptious joy,
Daih is Trombone Pete in suit o' raid,
Holdin' high wid pride his wooly haid,
 (Hum! Ti! Tum! Tum! Boom! Ti-Boom! Boom! Boom!
Git away an' gib dose anguls room!)

Lawdy! but dat music' stirs mah soul,
Mak' me think Ah see de streets ob gol';
Now Ah feel a-ticklin' in mah feet
Dat will set me dancin' on de street;
Glohry! Hallelujia! Heish yo' mouf!
Dat ban' sholy owns de livin' Souf.
Hooray! Keep it up, ol' Trombone Pete,
You hab won mah hea't an' won mah feet.

PLANTATION SERMON.

1.

Doan' you hyeah me preachin',
 Chillun in de valley?
Doan' you hyeah me 'spoundin',
 Chillun in de valley?
Freedom sh's a comin'
In de Savior's keeridge,
Ah kin hyeah it shoutin'
F'um de mouf ob cannons;
Oh, de robes am whituh

VISIONS OF THE DUSK.

Dan de light ob mawnin'
Oh, de songs am sweetuh
Dan de banjo's tummin',
Mighty am de gethrin'
Ob de wounded chillun,
Mighty am de buhstin'
F'um de th'oats ob singuhs.
Git yo' clo's a-ready,
Cleah yo' cotton patches,
Set yo' feet a-dancing'
In de Gospel mannah,
Ah kin hyeah de blowin'
Ob de golden trumpets.
Freedom's hitched huh hosses
An' she's drawin' nighuh.
Bury all yo' troubles,
Bury all yo' grievin's,
God hab hyeahed yo' prayin'—
Freedom's in de whirlwind,
An' we's in de valley.

THE PHANTOM RABBIT.

1.

Look, my weary brother, ere you die;
Night is here, and phantom nigh;
Soul of rabbit with the magic breath,
Soul of Life and foe of living Death.
    Ere we die, my brother, ere we die.

Visions of the Dusk.

2.

Look, my weary sister, ere we die;
O'er the hills the phantom shadows lie;
Rabibt ghostly soothes your aching fears,
Rabbit ghostly dries your endless tears,
  Ere we die, my sister, ere we die.

TO JEANNE ROBERT FOSTER.

Thy faith in me is comfort, friend unseen;
Tho' I am but a minstrel of the dusk,
Before my path thou strewest cloth of rose
That I may sing awhile my humble song.

S. COLERIDGE TAYLOR.

1.

Mute thy strings, O Israfel:
Quenched thy fire, and shrouded low
Men who marvelled at the spell
And the weird but dream borne glow
  Of thy master song.

2.

Israfel, no singers rise
Who can lift thy laurel crown,
Thou alone to glory rise—
Star of England's fair renown
  And the dusk man's hope.

VISIONS OF THE DUSK.

3.

When the Master came thou heard
Music woven of the night,
And, as soars a fleet winged bird,
Thou in melody made flight
    To the Throne of God.

4.

Will the meadows bloom again?
Will the lark in passion song
Lead us to his leafy den?
Will the day remain as long?
    Israfel has gone.

5.

Live to sing as he has sung,
Live to know the heart of God,
Live to speak an angel tongue
And to kiss the moistened sod
    O'er our Israfel.

Visions of the Dusk.

ETHIOPIA.

O minstrel lyre of ancient Ethiop,
Whose flaming song awoke the Orient,
O long forgotten harp, whose mouldering strings
Hath once enthralled the hearts of warriors,
I pray thee let my burning fingers press
Thee once again that I may sing my song
Ere from my veins the warmth of life hath flown.
O minstrel lyre, no longer do the kings
On couch of leopard skins await thy hour;
The Gods are dead, our ancient glory dust,
Our altars broken, and our people gone,—
Gone whence men quaff the wine of melting pot.
O, Libya, for thee the Prophet longs,
O Egypt, born of Sphinx and shadow forms,
O Ethiop, the flame of desert sands,
Thy hour! Thy hour! Oh, when shall come thy hour?

I touch the ancient lyre, and burning sing
The song of Ethiopia the Queen,
The song of her who sits among the gates,
Her eye upon the dawn of liberty and hope.

I.

The groves of Libya with perfume droop,
The dancing maidens, born of dusk and dew,
Before the flame their wierdest chants have raised,
The moon that lives for love and love alone

Visions of the Dusk.

From vale within the sky beholds the earth;
On throne of cedar, ophyr, and of gold
The jewelled monarch sits, a man of dusk,
Too opulent of war and cruelty,
Too drunk with power, too weak for noble deeds,
His star the strength that lives in mighty arms,
That sweeps before it all the tribes of earth
He is the morning of the human race,
The first sweet cup of wine existence drinks,
And on the altar luxury he falls,
A broken goblet in the hands of Time.
(Of such has been the human chronicle,
The Cæsars, Ptolemies, Alexanders fall,
Great Pompey is the dust of long ago,
And star swept Bonaparte hath met his doom.)
Behind a Northern Chariot the king
With chains of gold around his ebon neck
Must grace the triumph of his enemy,
His people must in slavery bend low,—
The moon of love hath died within the East.
A stranger walks within the grove enow;
But in the years to come that stranger falls
Before another.—So the will of God
Removes the nations, races, and the tribes,
Lest man should be the peer of God Himself.

II.

I hear the martial beat of long ago,
The clash of steel, the tread of Persian hordes.

Visions of the Dusk.

O Ethiop, how desolate thy shores!
How deep into oblivion thy star!
Thy children's children shall forget thy name,
Forget thy altars, and thy sacred fires,
F or from the parching sands of Araby,
Mohammed rides with death or Allah's law.
The wandering tribes of Abyssinia,—
From whence the Sheban queen her journey made,—
Alone survive the glory of the past,
But not the mandates of our ancient gods.
The haughty race that built the pyramids,
That chained the lion and the leopard cub,
With bleeding wounds are prostrate to the West;
In bondage to the priest of Christ and love
Exiled the men of dusk must dwell a day.
The pale and yellow ha ired from distant shores
Rob Ghana of her bronze and Congo land
Yields tortured slaves to grace a Christian age.
O, World Anew, from splendours barbaric,
From fields of cocoa and of drooping date,
From houses built of sunkist bamboo straw
Thou bringest fathers of a newer race,
Their wrists engyved, their souls in bitterness.
O Mighty Universal Diety,
Upon these exiles pour thy wond'rous love,
For sorrow shall be theirs and loneliness
Among a people who forget the name
Of star crowned Ethiop and Nubia.

Visions of the Dusk.

III.

The chains that man hath forged the heavens break,
Divine is liberty the slaves achieve;
And Hayti smoulders with the flames of dusk,
Her saviour loving Toussaint, prince of men.
The years may glide beyond the tide of time,
The stars may dim with age, and life grow faint,
But all the sons of men shall not forget
The Western Nazarene who died with love
For those whose treachery caused his death.
O Toussaint, may thy grave be ever green
With wreaths from all oppressed throughout the world,
May fifty thousand drums reveille roll,
A tribute to thy precious memory.
With thee the renaissance of Ethiop
Achieved, like other fires, was quenched awhile;
The cruel splendour Christophe embraced,
The anarchy that followed Citadels
Was not of thee, or thine, great Star of Dusk.
Thy message came to old Virginia's woods,
"Ah! Freemen shall we be", gaunt Turner cries
And with the courage of the patriot
He fought a day to give our land the glow
Of liberty, fraternity, and love.
He fought a day, and died a traitor's death,
But bright his halo, green his laurel crown.
Each blow for freedom struck is freedom's gain,
And Ethiop shall yet stretch forth her hand.

Visions of the Dusk.

IV.

When Night surrounds the slave, and hope lies cold,
The daytime breaks and Frederic is borne
On Fortune's tide to plead the cause of right.
Men marvel that a lowly son of dusk
Could move to tears the hardened soul of greed,
And crown his massive brow with laurel wreath.
His heart rejoiced when war destroyed the chains
That kept to earth his brothers of the dusk,
And when the sun of Freedom shone awhile
He marched abreast with Toil to save his race
Ah! hear the bells a-ringing through the world,
"The slave is free! Grim bondage dies to-night!"
O blessed war, that saved humanity,
That gave the men of dusk the freemen's right,
How many sons of Ethiop were thine!
How many fell with Shaw ere peace returned!
Their graves unknown, who strews for them sweet
                                          flowers?
Who keeps their memory with incense fresh?
How many when young Cuba, lashed by Spain,
A greater country saved, were lost at war!
No truer soldiers live than men of dusk,
No better lovers of the starry flag.
No hope is theirs but welfare of the world,
No honours for the fighters of the dusk,
Are these rewards, O great America?
Obscurity, oppression, bitter scorn,

Visions of the Dusk.

The right to serve, but never right to share.
Give us our liberty or give us death!

V.

And now that Freedom's orb so brightly burns
From crimson clay in old Virginia soil
Sweet Nature moulds another Washington;
Upon his brow she sets a flaming star,
Upon his lips the fire that never dies,
And smiles when men before his gospel bow,—
"The hand of toil alone will rule the world."
O Washington, may day upon us break!
May great America at last be free,
And true democracy where work is law
A common gift to all humanity.
Tuskegee's glory through the ages lives
The light that makes Columbia a queen
Among the toiling nations of the earth,
Tuskegee stands a stone in Jacob's dream,
A ladder leading to the Gates of Pearl,—
And Washington alone hath laid the stone.

VI.

There sits aloft among the jaspar gates
Far famed the brooding spirit of his race,
A gentle soul by grim injustice wracked
He looks in vain for hope, though he is hope.
O Ethiopia ,in him thy King,
Thy weaver of the vision glorious,
Thy lover begging for thy liberty.

Visions of the Dusk.

When Nature moulded him she chose a clay
So fine it could not bear a cruel storm;
But shaped his ponderous brow for laurel wreath.
In ages yet unborn the child of dusk
In reverence shall bow to Burghardt's name,
And all the world shall love a patriot.

VII.

O sons of Libya, thy name will live
The bearers of the Cross on Calvary;
Around thee wrapt the mantle of the dusk,
In thee the world will find another dawn,
Around thee shall the hour of twilight glow,
When day upon thee breaks a golden throne
Awaits thee in the land of rising sun,
Thy faith, thy deeds, thy love for fellow men
Shall be thy sceptre and thy coronet,
Before thee shall the vaunting nations bow
In reverence to crowned humility.

And thus I sing the song of Ethiop
Though I am dwelling in a stranger's land,
A lonely minstrel, born to serve and love
Throughout the world his fellows of the dusk.

DE CHU'CH.

'Way down de lane, behin' a row o' trees,
Whaih all de summah croons de softes' breeze

Visions of the Dusk.

De ol' plantashun chu'ch am shinin' white.
We da'kies lingah daih each Sund'y night,
A-shoutin' praise to Gawd an' Jesus, too.
We love de benches, made o' pine tree wood,
We love de place whaih all de elduhs stood
Each qua'tly meetin' day, a singin' himes
An' tellin' us erbout de good ol' times
W'en 'ligion was de only thing on earf.
De preachuh's haid widout an inch o' turf
Went waggin' 'way lak he's b'en set on fiah
"O Chillun, in de hebben libs de quiah
Ob dose who shaired de trubbles ob de Lawd,
Ob dose who found below de love ob Gawd.
Come throw yo' se'f befo' de Mussy Seat,
Come wash in Jesus blood yo' sinful feet.
De Son ob Man's de Shephud ob de fol',
De cripple lam' beneaf His cloak He hol'.
In Hebben He hab filled yo' honey dish,
Yo' comin' homewa'd's all dat He kin wish."
He hug de bible, an' de sistahs shout
A-puttin' all de debbils to de rout,
"Ol' Mount Moriah's lifted to de sky
An' anguls on de wing go flittin' by.
But w'en de deacon pass de wine an' braid
Each Christ'un soul in reverence hang his haid.
He am de chosen brothah ob de King,
An' low an' mounful lak he's sho' to sing,
"Ah want to meet mah Saviour face to face."
No, honey! all de worl' kin hol' no place

Visions of the Dusk.

Jes' lak de ol' plantashun chu'ch ob mine;
It am de manshun ob de lowly folk,
It am de spot whaih Gawd Himself hab spoke,
It am de only place to shake de han',
An' know dat you's as good as any man.
Oh, dat's de place fu' me to live an' die,
Beneaf de Mussy ob de Saviour's eye.

DE MULE.

1.

Oh, sweet de wa'blin' ob de mockin' bu'd,
A singin' to de moon his song ob love,
Oh, sweet de voice ob Dinah in de dew
A singin', "Honey, you's mah tu'tle dove";
Oh, sweet de angel on de golden street
A singin', "Satan sho's a mighty fool,"
But nevah hab ah hu'd a voice so sweet
As Jasper's brayin', an' he's mah good ol' mule.

2.

It soun's jes' lak de thundah in de sky
A rollin' swiftly down to Jordan's stream,
It soun's jes' lak de cannons in de war
A makin' ob dis worl' a mighty dream
It soun's jes' lak de shoutin' ob de men
Dat lapped wid Gideon f'un out de pool,
It soun's as if de sweetes' note ob all
Am dat dat come f'um jes' a plain ol' mule.

Visions of the Dusk.

QUESTIONS.

1.

"Whaih's de twilight, Mammy Lou?"
" 'Way beyond de drippin' dew,
Whaih de angels run an' hide
Happy by ol' Jawdon's tide."

2.

Whaih's de moonlight, Mammy Lou?"
"Whaih de day's a-slippin' thoo,
An' de lamp called Lub's tu'ned high—
Nevah kin de moon go dry."

3.

"Whaih's de sunlight, Mammy Lou?"
"Why Ah thought you allus knew
Dat yo' hea't's de wahm sunlight
An' yo' love's de moon o' night."

LYRICS OF LOVE.
LYRIC ONE.

1.

When in Slumberland the dreams go forth
To my heart a darling maiden comes,
Stardust are her eyes, her lips love flame,
And an angel tune she softly hums.

VISIONS OF THE DUSK.

II.
Never 'neath the dwelling place of God,
Never by the lake or by the sea,
Was a man so blest as I am blest
With the love that Clara gives to me.

III.
Oh, my heart will burn for ages long
From a fever that will never die,
For in Slumber land an elfin rogue
Poured his magic lotion on my eye.

LYRIC TWO.

I.
This is the hour, my love, the hour of tryst;
The earth is sleeping in the cool of dusk,
The lily-of-the valley nods and sways,
The air is drooping with the perfumed musk.

II.
Ah! open wide, my love, thy garden gate;
Eftsoons the ancient moon will ply her barge,
For thee I bring sweet Cupid's rosary,
To thee a book of kisses do I charge.

III.
When Eden's glory thrived, fair Eve was won
At such an hour as this, our trysting hour,
And burning Romeo, when Night was Queen,
Enthralled young Juliet within her bower.

Visions of the Dusk.

IV.

Then blest be every hour that Love holds sway,
And sweet the roses of the eventide.
Then blest the crucial moment of this life,
When down the stream of passion sweethearts glide.

LYRIC THREE.

I.

Sweet pigeon carrier upon my roof,
Oh, tell me, tell me how my lover fares!
Last night to war he marched, his breast aglow,
Within his heart his troubled country's cares.

II.

"O lovely maiden, many tears shall fall
Ere to thy bosom shall thy lover fly;
Beneath the Belgian moon, in bloody death,
With thousands does your ardent lover lie."

III.

Oh, woe is me! The moon and stars have died,
No more for me the dance on village green;
My couch is spread upon the meadowland,
Six feet of darkness 'neath the churchyard green.

LYRIC FOUR.

I.

Returned am I, my trusted sweetheart dead;
Upon her lonely grave Golgotha's Cross,

Visions of the Dusk.

Upon the stone the dreaded legend "Gone!"
Upon the mound a spray of hawthorn moss.

II.

She went when Springtime kissed the sleeping earth,
Too soon to fall the prey of brooding grief.
For one who shall be lonely through the years,
She gave the God of Death a life too brief.

III.

I care not now what woes may fall on me,
The sorrow infinite is ever mine.
Beside the river Lethe I shall muse,
But never taste the sweetness of the wine.

WHEN APRIL COMES.

1.

When April comes as April will
No more in eagerness my soul
Shall cringe and ask that thou shalt hear
My humble songs, my melody;
No more shall I go panting forth,
Close 'pon me wild hounds hot o' breath.
For in the April time my hour
Shall dawn, the hour of tranquil dusk;
And when the earth is all anew,
Revived by hope the springtime grants,
I know that I shall drift away,
Where poets have their holiday.

VISIONS OF THE DUSK.

2.

Oh, heavy is this life of mine,
And I, a broken reed 'mongst men.
I lived a plaintive melody,
Unsung, unloved, unknown, unwept.
I loved as every youth will love,
But she on whom I poured my love
Was not for me,—I know not why,
I dreamed as every youth should dream,
But all my dreams to air have changed,
And now that I am going forth
To break my wand I breathe a prayer
That those, my brothers of the dusk,
Shall not forget that I have lived
But in the tide of love shall drop
Upon my lonely grave a rose,
For one who lived his life for them.

THE CLINGING KISS.

I.

The earth awhirl,
Sweetheart, I wander far
Adown the crowded street,
Upon my burning lips
The clinging kiss.

II.

A thousand years
May sear this life of mine,

VISIONS OF THE DUSK.

But in my memory
I hold one treasure dear,
   The clinging kiss.

III.

A thousand caravans
May bear a wealth untold,
The stones of India
Will pale beside my gem,
   The clinging kiss.

IV.

O wondrous love,
That burns to ash my heart,
Give back to me that hour
She placed upon my lips
   The clinging kiss.

EULOGY ON THE FAIRIES.

Oh, where are the fairies now?
Poverty, poverty,
Hast thou robbed the merry elves
Of their right to live and breathe?
Barren is the Southland now,
There the dusk men writhe in pain;
Barren is old Amsterdam,
There each year we offer babes
On the shrine of Gold and Greed;
Barren is Killarney's green,

Visions of the Dusk.

Erin's fairies pine away
For the light of liberty;
From his cave hoar Merlin cries,
"Self! Self! Self! hath killed the elves,
Self, the basest of the God;
Nevermore, nevermore,
Shall the airy creatures rove
With their magic caps and bells,
Spreading wonder everywhere;
Fairy night hath turned to day
Moonlight fades, the stars are dead,
Naught can bring the fairies back,
Naught save Love, the long lost Love,
Bring him from his secret lodge,
Crown his brows, and let him reign,
Seat him on the Throne of Years
To the strain of minstrel lyre.
For the fairies must return
Ere the twilight of the earth."

Where are the fairies now?
Titania and Oberon,
And Puck, who changed the night to day
And slept beneath the rose hued sun?

Visions of the Dusk.

MEMORIES.

1.
When at evening in the vale I walk,
Wrapt in memories of dear Lucille;
When among the violets I lie,
All my hours of love before me steal.

2.
Earth and heaven was this maid to me,
And her voice the song of lark and wren;
Now that she hath left my heart I know
Through the love of women God makes men.

3.
If in distant countries I should dwell
With a people strange and proudly cold,
I would always see my long lost love
In the heart of dying marigold.

WHEN MY BONNIE DANCES.

1.
When my Bonnies dances earth is mine,
And a thousand kingdoms I can see;
I am thrilled with joy and love and hope,
And my sweetheart's goodness comes to me.
In her eye the vision Hellas knew,
In her step the dream o' wanton Rome;
And in garb o' white she mocks a queen,
As she finds within my heart a home.

Visions of the Dusk.

2.

When my Bonnie dances fields are green,
Blood stained roses bloom, and asphodel;
And Beloved walks awhile with me,
Where I wooed her in a lonely dell.
Rivers feel the warmth o' sunlit gaze,
Sweet canary sings within the grove,
And I nod as music sways my nymph
Where the sprites of Nature lightly rove.

3.

When m yBonnie dances, music's stream,
Silv'ry white as glows the old moon's breast,
Flows into the liquid veins of Youth,
Warmer than a maiden's fond caress;
And the spheres of Heaven, all attuned,
To the rhythmic measure sets the world,
While the flowers that sleep on eve of snow
From their beds their petals gay unfurl.

4.

Oh, my Bonnie, thou hast won a crown,
Love and worship from the world of youth,
And through dancing graceful thou hast carved
On our hearts the magic legend TRUTH;
Long may Bonnie live and drink the sweets
Men call living, God above call life,
Long may Bonnie live and never know
Woe and sorrow, bitterness and strife.

Visions of the Dusk.

MARY ON AUGUST THE FIRST.
1.
I heard the voice of Mary in the cool of evening:
"Oh why the devastation of the golden wheatlands?
Oh why the burning of the villages and homelands?
My shrines are broken, and my statue changed to bullets,
My lowly Son is once again a God rejected,
And all my children walk the way of life in darkness."
2.
I bowed to earth my head, and thus I answered Mary:
"That we might gather in the vineyard empty glory,
That we might wear a ribbon and a wreath of laurel,
We hurl to Hell a million souls and go our way,
The laughing demons of an age whose God is sleeping,
Forgetful of the women and the little children,
And thrice forgetful of the chariot of progress."

DOUGLAS.
He came when tyranny was ripe, a torch
That lit the darkened avenue of hope,
He came from cabin, ragged, poor, and starved,
And walked among the honoured of the earth.
His cry the cry of Moses to the King,
"Oh, let my people go, thou freeborn host,
For God hath heard their cry; they must be free."

Visions of the Dusk.

He walked not shrouded, but with manhood stride,
The morning of a people long oppressed,
He stood within the palace of the King
And cried, "Give them their rights; they must be free.
These lowly folks,—my brothers, ay, thine, too
Let not a democratic people cringe
To selfish idols, childish prejudice
Let not the future ages note this land
That broke the chains Hanover's puppet forged
Enslaves and keeps enslaved a helpless race,
Whose hand has never struck the stars and stripes."
Ah! there was Phillips; there was Sumner, too,
With Lowell, Garrison, and Whittier,
And Brown, whose noble life Virginia took,
And Stowe, wohse pen awoke the slumbering North;
But none of Afric line as bold as he,
As fiery and inveterate of speech,
As monumental of the intellect
A man of dusk may have, tho' born in chains—
A worthy peer for such a company.
When chaos ruled, and freedmen knew not where
The star of fortune would abide with them
This Douglas, dauntless as the wind of March,
As shepherd guides his sheep o'er stony crags
He guided long his race, all bruised and torn,
And faltering because the night was dark;
Until he heard the still small voice of Death
And drifted down the endless stream of Time.

VISIONS OF THE DUSK.

O Dougles, thou hast left a heritage
To those whose brows are pierced by thorned crowns
And from thy couch in green Elysium
Where thou and Sumner and the laurelled Grant,
And Ingersoll and Lincoln watch the tide,
Thy voice comes down to us, thy bleeding sheep.
And these thy words, O Prophet of the Dusk!
"Go on, my Race, the sun will rise again,
The Night will fade as darkness ever fades.
No race can always bend beneath the yoke,
For 'tis a truth the wrath of those oppressed
Will break the reins, and drink of liberty.
Be valiant, true, and know not cowardice
And live so that both friend and foe may say,
"Oh they were great in adversity
But greater in the hour of jubilee!"

Thus speaks our Douglas from his grave, and we
Should heed his mighty voice, lest we should fail.

OL' AGE.

1.

Mandy, we is growin' ol' an' gray,
F'om us life is ebbin' eb'ry day;
We is nigh de time when angels call
"Come to Jesus in de Golden Hall."
We have he'ped each othah 'long de road,
Totin' on ouah backs de heavy load;

VISIONS OF THE DUSK.

We have made dis livin' lak a song
Dat is sung in Heaven by de throng.

2.

Eyes am growin' dim, an' bones do ache,
Han's dat wu'ked so ha'd begin to shake,
Pickannines grown an' gone daih way,—
Life is lak a meller autumn day.
Nuffin' but de sleepin' an' de dreams,
Nuffin' but de place whaih twilight gleams,
Nuffin' do but pick de banjo strings
Whaih de vine upon de cabin clings.

THE WRAITHIE'S MESSAGE.

1.

Last night before my window came
A wraithie bathed in living flame,
"I am a herald of the night,
I am a lonely, lonely wight.

2.

"Beside the sea a maiden dwells,
Her voice the sound of lighthouse bells,
Her eyes the green of starlit sea,
Her soul a dwelling place for thee.

3.

"Good dreamer, I have touched her heart,
With burning song I touched her heart

VISIONS OF THE DUSK.

And now her dreams are all of thee—
This maiden by the deathless sea."
4.
Oh, lead me hence, good elf of night,
Oh, lead to her signal light;
For I am weary of my dreams,
Long weary of my feverish dreams.

WASHIN' DAY.
1.
Weddah beats de dickens,
Heat wid sweat am mixin';
Pappy wants some bac'n,
But he's sh' mistaken
   On dis washin' day.
2.
Baby in de grasses,
Mouf all smeared wid 'lasses.
Ain't he mostes' cunnin'?
Look-a-daih he's runnin'!
   Knows no washin' day.
3.
Who am dat a-hidin'?
Boy, you quit yo' slidin'.
Heah, you lazy sinnah,
Come an' tuhn dat wringah,
   Dis am washin' day.

VISIONS OF THE DUSK.

4.

Lawd! dese suds am splashin',
Makin' noise dat's crashin';
Put dose clo's tuh soakin',
Asmy's got me chokin'
    On dis washin' day.

5.

No, Ah ain't a shu'kin',
Jes' tuh keep f'um wu'kin';
It's de robin's singin',
Sweetes' freedom bringin'
    F'um dis washin' day.

AT THE SHRINE OF MARY.

1.

"Mary Mother, we are twining flowers,
Flowers gleaned from the meadows, pure with love,
That thy golden head may wear a crown
Whiter than the bosom of a dove".
Children mine, entwine no flowers for me;
In the Kingdom gleams a thousand flowers,
Richer than the fairest blooms of earth,
Purer than a maiden's sacred hours.

2.

Give instead the treasures of thy heart,
Give instead a garland of thy deeds,
Shower thy mercies on the lowly folk,

Visions of the Dusk.

Who must ever dwell among the weeds;
London beggars cry, and Ireland starves,
Naked Hindustan is pinched for food,
Give them, my children, give to them;
God conceived them, they are Mary's brood.

3.

Give the poor oppressed the burning lamp
Liberty hath held for ages long,
Give my sisters weapon for their wrongs
That the latter days may glow with song;
Let the bleeding sons of Ethiop,
Let my kinsmen, seed of Israel,
Hear no more the word of hate and scorn,
Feel no more the fire of living Hell.

4.

"Mary Mother, we are twining flowers,
Flowers gleaned from the meadows pure with love,
That thy golden head may wear a crown
Whiter than the bosom of a dove;
Love the petal, Love the calyx too,
Love of man and love of womankind,
Betterment for all who walk in pain—
Those are flowers our hearts have long enshrined."

VISIONS OF THE DUSK.

A PILGRIM OF THE DUSK.
1.
Out of the dusk came I,
A strong man I, song sheafed,
My star humanity,
My brow with sorrow leafed;
I saw the Giant of Love
Upon the Northern Pole,
"I know thee not", he cried,
"I know no flame bound soul."
2.
Oh, lonely is my road,
No merry pilgrim here.
The darkness is my shroud,
My drink a bitter tear;
Tho' Love hath passed me by
I see the After-Glow,
And when my day is done
The Angels I shall know.

DEATH.

When from Eden's land we stray
In the morningtime of life
God in pity kisses us
And around us sheds His love — — —
Men have named this wonder Death.

Visions of the Dusk.

WARNING.

Keep yo' eyes ez tight ez tight kin be,
    Mammy's erroun', Mammy's erroun';
Lock yo' lips, an' lock 'em wid a key,
    Mammy's erroun', Mammy's erroun';
In huh han's a great big hic'ry stick,
An' de fustes' one she gibs a lick,
How de rascal sma't an' how he yell,
How de uddas grin, fu' know day well,
    Mammy's erroun', Mammy's erroun'.

2.

Doan' you sass, o' hu't de preachuh man,
    Mammy's erroun', Mammy's erroun'.
Doan' you try tuh fill his hat wid san',
    Mammy's erroun', Mammy's erroun';
Bestes' close yo' eyes an' say yo' pra'rs,
Stiffen up an' git yo' Sunday a'rs,
Pass de preachuh man de chicken bres'
An' be listnin' close tuh all he says,
    Mammy's erroun', Mammy's erroun'.

DECLARATION.

1.

I love the world and all therein:
The panting, darkened souls who seek
A brighter light, a sweeter hope,

Visions of the Dusk.

From those who drink the bubbling wine
And eat the flesh of tender fowl;
I love the pampered son af wealth,
And pour on him my pity's oil,
This world our God hath made for all,—
The East, the West, the black, the white,
The rich, the poor, the wise, the dumb,—
And even beasts may share the fruit;
No prison wall, but sunlight's glow,
No rods of steel, but arms of love,
For all that creep and walk and strive
And wear upon their countenance
Creation's mark, the kiss of God.

TURN DOWN THE LAMP.

Turn down the lamp; my life is done.
The fitful moments drift to ease—
Rosemary for the dreams that died,
And mignonette for cherished hopes.
Turn down the lamp; my soul gains life;
I rise above the narrow pale
Of cities bought with gold and slime,
I spread my sorrow strengthened wings
Above the armies of the world,
In quest of kingdoms built in youth.
The hour of death that men call life
Is closing as a troubled dream,
The flame within my lamp is low,

Visions of the Dusk.

I seek eternal liberty,
The freedom of the endless sky.
Good nurse, enfold my arms,
And cool the fever of my brow,
My hour has come, turn down the lamp.

COMIN' HOME.

1.

Oh, Ah hyeahs de ol' tahm bells a-ringin',
    Comin' home! Comin' home!
Sweetuh dan de angel hahp de singin',
    Comin' home! Comin' home!
Bu'dens dat Ah's toted fifty yeahs
Ah has laid away wid foolish teahs,
To de skies Ah raise mah weary eyes
An' to Dinah honey long Ah cries
    Comin' home! Comin' home!

2.

Oh, Ah hyeahs de ol' tahm folk a-callin'
    Comin' home! Comin' home!
Cross de Jawdon shadders gently fallin'
    Comin' home! Comin' home!
Down de stream dey float de ol' flat boat,
Songs ob sorrer comin' f'om daih th'oat,
Dey is gwine to tote mah soul away
Whaih de moonlight tu'ns de night to day,
    Comin' home! Comin' home!

VISIONS OF THE DUSK.

L'ENVOI.

The dreamer nods, and honeyed sleep
His eyelids woo; his day is done.
No more the vision burns his soul,
But lives within his memory.
Her shadow mantle Evening drops;
The bee is drowsy on the vine;
From heart of rose the pollen drips,
And dripping blinds the fairy's eye.
Across the surging tide of Night
Comes reasonant the voice of God
"Oh Love!—True love is best of all;
It lives ... it lives beyond the years."